# Steel City Setlist

# Steel City Setlist

*Navigating the Pittsburgh Music Scene*

Maleena Dominick

Steel City Setlist: Navigating the Pittsburgh Music Scene

By Maleena Dominick



First Edition

Cover design by Sharon Dominick

ISBN: 978-1-257-56669-3
Imprint: Lulu.com

*Printed in the United States of America*

*For the artists who wrote the soundtrack of this city, the venues that keep their doors open, and the community that makes Pittsburgh loud.*

*This book is for you.*

# TABLE OF CONTENTS

# INTRODUCTION

The Pittsburgh music scene is just as complex and detailed as the streets that weave throughout the city. Its rich history, diversity, and variety make it impossible to capture all that this community has to offer. “The kids in the Hill District have a completely different scene than the kids in the South Side, or in Lawrenceville, or in Garfield, or in Brookline,” says Jeff Betten of Misra Records and Hellbender Vinyl. “Not to mention that the metal heads probably don't know much about what the hip-hop heads are doing, and vice versa. It's complicated and messy, but absolutely everyone around the world agrees that Pittsburgh punches above its weight class when it comes to music.”

This book is an autoethnography of the Pittsburgh music scene. Autoethnography is a style of writing and research on a subculture that combines the writer's personal experiences with qualitative conclusions about cultural, social, and political themes. Over 30 musicians across a dozen subscenes and genres contributed their perspectives to this project, offering first-hand accounts of the different experiences in this large community. While significant amounts of research went into this work, it is in no way a complete reflection of every corner of Pittsburgh's music scene. This city's musical landscape is so vast that a lifetime would barely suffice to explore every venue, genre, and musician in depth.

*Secret Tunnel setlist*

# CHAPTER ONE

I run down the narrow stairs, my heart beating with anticipation. I had just finished curling my freshly dyed purple hair and putting on my makeup. That was the final step in transforming myself from everyday Maleena to stage Maleena—the most real version of myself. The lights dim as the previous band gather their gear and leave the stage. I sling my prized possession—my sparkly Kiesel 5-string bass—over my shoulder and brace myself for the experience I'm about to have. The stage I am about to perform on is one of the best in Pittsburgh. I have seen so many of my favorite touring bands and artists play at Mr. Smalls, but tonight is all about local musicians.

I peek around the corner to see that the venue is full of people. There are a few familiar faces, but mostly strangers in the crowd. I take a deep breath. I'm not nervous, but adrenaline is pumping through my veins. The house music ends, and our intro music begins to play. Excitement fills the entire venue. Nolan walks out onto the stage first and is greeted with a cheer. I make sure I have everything I need. My heart is beating out of my chest. It's go time.

I run out onto the stage, and the crowd explodes. I look out into the audience, taking in the feeling of having hundreds of eyes looking at me to put on a show. It feels like I am in slow motion, like a scene from a movie. Then Chip—my dad, our frontman—joins us, and the room roars once again. The lights, sound, and energy wrap around me from every corner of the venue. As soon as our intro music ended, we launched into

"Paying Back the Devil," and I got choked up as I saw the crowd go wild. I almost let a tear fall. Not out of fear, but out of joy. Out of a surreal, victorious feeling that I was finally living out the real experience of what I had always dreamed of. These people showed up for me, just a local musician.

*Beasts of the Burgh III at Mr. Small's Theater*

*Sharon Dominick Photography*

This moment is what being a local musician is all about. It’s not about fame, or stepping on others to try to get to the top—it's about connection. It’s about putting in a lot of work, playing to half-empty rooms, promoting, and networking just for the chance to have a night like this. Being a part of the local music scene means building something real with the people who care the most. It means sharing the stage with friends, supporting each other’s projects, watching bands go from opener to headliner, and most importantly, showing up. It’s more than just musicians. It is a network of artists all chasing the same dream together.

**Mr. Smalls Theatre: Production Schedule**
**Saturday, March 22, 2025**

**Headline Load In:** 3:00 PM
**Support Load In:** 3:00 PM
**Production Load In:** 4:00 PM
**Sound Check:** Following Load In.
**Doors:** 7:00 PM

**Travel and Parking**
**Headline Travel:**
**Support Travel:**
**Headline Parking:**
**Support Parking:**

**Set Times**

| | |
|---|---|
| **XDB** | **10:15 PM - 10:45 PM** |
| **Never Say Die** | **9:30 PM - 10:00 PM** |
| **Chip and The Charge Ups** | **8:45 PM - 9:15 PM** |
| **Griffen Handshake** | **8:00 PM - 8:30 PM** |

**Curfew:** 11:30 PM
**Bus Call:**

**Notes**

**Promoter/Venue Staff:**
Please direct any questi[illegible] appropriate party or parties below:
**Box Office Rep:**
**Promoter Rep:**
**FOH Engineer:**
**Monitor Engineer:**
**Lighting Designer:**
**House GM:**
**Security:**
**Police:**
**Ages:**

**Headline Contacts**
Please direct any questions to the appropriate party or parties below:
**Tour Manager:** Chip & The Charge Ups
**Production Manager :** XDB
**FOH Engineer**
**Lighting Designer :** Never Say Die

*Beasts of the Burgh III production schedule*

The Pittsburgh music scene is its own society, with its own set of rules, rulers, hardships, and shortcuts. If you're just joining this community for the first time, the connections you make are invaluable to you. Having someone's back often means they will have yours when you need it. However, that may not always be the case. There tends to be a bit of exclusivity from a handful of bands, artists, and promoters that often act like they are too good to support you when you're at the bottom of the ladder. That might pose a rather large roadblock, but beware: there are many more. Possibly the biggest problem you will face is the fact that venues are dropping like flies. Getting a gig is already difficult as it is for bands who have been around for years, simply due to the lack of places to play. Luckily, there is a remedy for getting the recognition you deserve. Pittsburgh is full of opportunities for local musicians to promote themselves. From huge music festivals to open mics to opportunities for local music on radio airplay, there is always a way to make sure your music is heard.

IRE SET
10-25-25
WHEN WE WERE DEAD

1. BLOOD LUST
2. SHALLOW GRAVE
3. REFLECTIONS
4. RED INK
5. LOST YOUR FAITH
6. MARIONETTE
7. BROKEN HEARTS DON'T BEAT
8. LAID TO REST
9. DRUM SOLO
10. SMILE AND WATCH IT BURN
11. PARIS GREEN

*Ire setlist*

# PEOPLE IN THE SCENE

My heart sinks as the rain starts falling rapidly. I guess our chance to perform on the main stage is gone. The Deutschtown Music Festival has been happening for a few years at this point. My band had played this same festival a few times in previous years, but this time, in 2022, was our first time getting a time slot on the main stage. We get back in the car and begin the wait. As the rain and time pass by, we finally get a message from the organizer of the festival. He tells us that, unfortunately, 3 bands, including mine, got rained out and would not be able to perform on the main stage. Thankfully, he got us a time slot performing at a small bar around 1:00 am. Though it's not as epic as playing the main stage at 5:00 pm, I am so grateful that all the hard work we put into this show wasn't going to be for nothing.

The rain clears up, and other bands get to start performing again. We walk around and check out a few other bands, knowing that there are still a good 7 hours left until we will finally get our chance to perform. I get to see some of my friends' bands and check out some new artists I'd never heard of before. There's no doubt that Pittsburgh is full of talent. That is one of the best parts about these kinds of festivals. Finally, after seeing an amazing assortment of bands, we head over to the bar where we are performing. We have all our gear ready to go—guitars, basses, amps. The only thing we do not have is a drum kit. There's a band that offered to let the other bands use their drum kit for their performances. The band that performs before us, the ones who volunteered to share their drum kit, begin packing up and leaving. Panic begins to wash over all of us. "We were told you were backlining the drum kit."

"I'm going home, my wife has work in the morning," the drummer says, removing the drums from the back of the small bar.

None of us can believe this is happening right now. My band was set to perform in 15 minutes, and the drum kit we were supposed to use was being taken away from us. Not only that, but there is supposed to be one more band on after my band. I try to wrap my mind around this situation. Why would this band offer to share their drum kit, but take it away right before my band goes on? It feels like a personal attack. I feel rage wash over me like I never have before.

Here's the thing about Pittsburgh. Someone will *always* have your back.

A miracle walks our way—Joe Palermo, a friend that my dad had known from the music scene for well over 15 years. Whether it is by a lucky coincidence or by the power of God himself, Joe just so happens to have a drum kit. He is more than willing to let us borrow it—to help a fellow musician in their time of need. Because of his kindness to us that day, we were able to perform our show, despite every factor pointing to us not getting our chance.

*Chip & the Charge Ups, Broom, Hollow North*
*Sharon Dominick Photography*

The duality of the Pittsburgh music scene is rooted in its people—some will shut you out while others will go out of their way to lift you up. There are so many people in this music scene, all who play many different roles.

Obviously, there are artists and musicians. They make up the majority. Then there are engineers and producers. These people are the reason that the quality of recorded music coming out of the local scene is top-tier. Then we have the promoters. These are the people who organize shows and book the talent. Whether you love or hate them, they are a necessary element to put on an event. And finally, but most importantly, there are the supporters. The fans, friends, parents, colleagues, and even other musicians who come to shows, listen to music, and share the word about local talent. There would be no scene without support from people who care deeply about local music.

"There is a tight-knit **community** of musicians that want to help you," says Nolan Allen, drummer of pop-punk band Chip & the Charge Ups. "And over the years I've learned there's many different communities of these musicians. I used to think it was just one big community, but there's a lot of different niches."

*Nolan Allen of Chip & the Charge Ups*

*Sharon Dominick Photography*

Looking at the Pittsburgh music scene from the outside may look like one big group, but there are so many different outlets and avenues within the scene. These ‘niches’ are not even necessarily defined based on the genre each band or artist plays.

From my experience in the music scene, I have experienced many different niches. In my band, we have been part of the Rock for Life Concert Series—the community within just that one specific event is a well-oiled machine. The concert series typically consists of multiple benefit events, raising money for a specific child with healthcare needs. This subscene consists mostly of hard rock bands but does have a good bit of variety. Within my solo music, I am a part of the AcoustiCafe subscene. AcoustiCafe is the weekly open mic hosted at Mr. Smalls Funhouse. The environment there has so much diversity in genres and people but typically consists of high-level solo performers and songwriters.

Regardless of what subscene you get involved in, there will always be people waiting to welcome you with open arms. Cody Kulesa, drummer of 2000’s emocore cover band Never Say Die, says, “It's starting to become family-oriented, no matter what genre [of] music you're in.” The people you collaborate with truly become family, and Cody is a great example.

Cody has been working to provide opportunities for musicians in the community for many years. He’s not only an excellent musician but a great promoter as well. For the last few years, he has hosted several shows, including the annual “When We Were Dead” Halloween festival at 31 Sports Bar. He goes above and beyond to ensure that every band performing has the best possible experience. This ranges from decorating the stage and venue, creating a custom video to be projected on the screen behind each band, to simply making sure every single musician who performs gets paid. He has given amazing opportunities to my band—playing in new venues to new friendly faces. And because of this connection, we have his back. In February, his band needed a bassist to fill in for a show.

Cody and the other members of Never Say Die have been wonderful and welcoming to me in numerous ways, so it made it very easy for me to step up and help them out when they needed it most. Getting to play with them was not only saving their show, but also an exciting performance opportunity for me to get to play with incredibly talented musicians. Eventually, this led to me joining the band—something I would have never considered, until I experienced how the closeness of playing with strangers turns you into family.

*Alex Ribeau and Cassie Kulesa of Never Say Die*

*Sharon Dominick Photography*

It's not hard to see the love that the people of the scene have for their community. There are even a handful of songs written by musicians about the scene that reflect the sense of belonging that the scene brings.

"*Who I am, where I belong, made obvious when I sang along,*" from the song *Understatement* by punk band Understatement and Bala Rise.

"*Then I found this scene, it opened up my eyelids. There were others wearing colors like me. Their arms were open to love the broken. This is where I'm meant to be. I never wanna leave here. You can lock the door, won't shed tears. Cause this is where I fit in. I don't wanna go home,*" from *Where I Fit In* by my pop-punk band, Chip & the Charge Ups.

Both of these songs' lyrics reflect the way the Pittsburgh music scene is a welcoming environment. The sentiment of "where I belong" and "where I fit in" are perfect representations of the scene. It is a place where misfits and outcasts find solidarity.

Many amazing people in the scene will want to help out each member of this family of thousands of musicians. “Everybody seems to know everybody, but there's always a new band to check out,” says Tony Willoe, multi-instrumentalist and music gear expert. Tony, who has been a musical instrument salesperson for the last 15 years, has met thousands of musicians in Pittsburgh. He meets people who are just getting started with their musical journey daily.

I was a customer of his since I was 10 years old, stopping in his store to pick out my very first instrument. Working in the field he does, he knows truly how many musicians are out there in the scene working daily to achieve the shared dream we all have. Even for people who have been in the scene for decades, they are still making new connections daily.

The scene is so big that, even as a new musician, you will have an easy time finding the community where you fit in. There are endless possibilities for **collaboration**.

I started attending the AcoustiCafe open mic in 2022 and made a lot of friends and connections there. One person I met was Brad Yoder. He is an extremely talented multi-instrumentalist and singer-songwriter. He is the one guy that you never want to perform after at the open mic, just because he's *that* good. When I was finishing up writing a song in 2024, I decided the song needed a saxophone line. Knowing Brad was a skilled saxophonist, I sent him a message asking if he'd be willing to help me. Later that week, I was at his recording studio, and he ended up writing and recording a saxophone solo with multiple parts for my song. The song turned out even more amazing than I could have imagined, and I owe a lot of credit to him for the work that he did. Building connections like that with the most talented people you could ever meet is the reason the Pittsburgh music scene has become as big as it is.

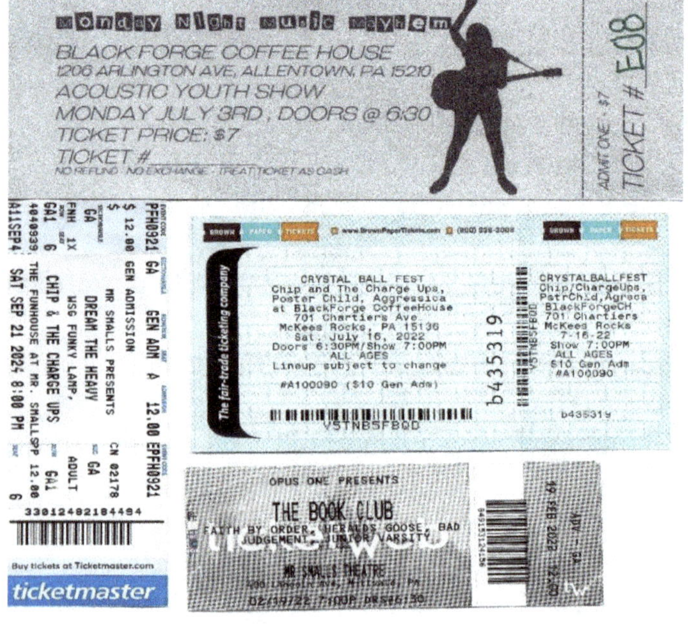


*Local show tickets*

With there being so many bands within the scene, this can also lead to a ton of **competition**. Music alone has competition. “You are not just competing with other bands that might be playing the same night, but you're competing with every single entertainment alternative that someone has,” says Chip Dominick, my dad and frontman of Chip & the Charge Ups.

There are two types of competition in the music scene. There is created competition, like battle of the bands, songwriting competitions, and rap battles. The other kind of competition is natural competition, which is just the result of having a music scene that is so large.

“If we're both playing on the same night, people can only come see one of us, right?” says Mike McInnes, guitarist of pop-punk band Old Neon. “There are definitely people that are more worried about that aspect of it, like trying to 'win' those sorts of things." Mike understands this type of competition well, as his band often competed for sets at big festivals, one of which being Four Chord Music Festival. He once again points out that the opportunities his band had gotten have all been the result of the close connections and friendships he's made in the scene, and the trust and credibility that he has earned.

There are endless possibilities of what to do on a weekend in Pittsburgh. There are sports games, bars, clubs, and endless opportunities to be entertained. Going to see a local band perform is just one of the many options that someone may have. And if a person does decide to see a local band, there are still many options for them to choose from. There aren't as many venues as there used to be, but there are so many bands.

For a fan to choose to come support your band in particular, not only over all of the other bands performing, but over all the other possible things to do—that in itself is an accomplishment.

As a musician in the scene, you will be competing for fans' attention, venues' attention, and promoters' attention. When you want to book a show, finding a venue that has openings will be very difficult. Many venues are booked out months in advance on the weekends. It is essential to book ahead for several reasons, but securing a date at a local venue will ensure that you can. As for playing a local festival, there will be several hundred bands applying to play. Millvale Music Festival, despite having over 300 bands perform annually, has to turn down hundreds of applicants. It can be easy to view this type of competition as a form of rejection.

Competition in the scene can be a double-edged sword. You can let it feel like a failure if you don't get your desired result, or you can use it to motivate you to create something more amazing. These factors don't necessarily create a strictly win-or-lose situation in the scene. The nature of this competition is not malicious, but just the natural consequence of being a part of something so large.

Though competition can be a motivator for a lot of artists, providing drive to put on the most anticipated show of the night, it can also create **conflict** between musicians.

"Friendly competition is something I've always liked," says Arnold Hullenbaugh, who plays drums for Arcane Haven, Ire, and Neverwake. "Whenever it turns into beef and unnecessary drama, it's something that just happens and I do not want to be a part of."

There is a lot of gatekeeping within the scene. Some bands or promoters are *only* willing to collaborate with their friends and aren't open to working with others in the scene. This can foster toxicity and hurt feelings where a sense of alliance and compassion are needed. Every musician is putting in all of their work and effort in the scene with the same goal: the hope that people will enjoy their music.

*Guitar Zack setlist*

Musicians don't always offer support, and in some cases, they may even be intentionally discouraging. With a music scene as big as Pittsburgh's, there is bound to be tension, no matter how hard you try to avoid it. Country artist Nathan King shared that while the country music scene isn't openly hostile, there's often a lack of collaboration between events. Reflecting on his transition from metal to country, he noted that the rock scene had a stronger sense of camaraderie. He says what he misses the most about the rock scene is that "we were all cheering for each other. And that's what I'm trying to do still."

Many challenges are rooted in localism and gatekeeping, which can block the potential for growth and new collaborations. A lot of artists and organizers tend to remain within their genre-specific circles, booking only their friends or familiar acts. This eliminates possibilities of "genre cross-pollination," which leads to creative expansion. The "general herding of one genre and social cliques," as Paul Dean Price III of Dream the Heavy puts it, prevents the scene from operating as a diverse yet united force.

Gatekeeping takes on various forms, from exclusive show curation to resistance against new ideas or outside perspectives. A notable example occurred when a consultant from Austin, Texas—a major music city—was brought in to create a game plan for improving the Pittsburgh scene. A group of hecklers "basically shut the whole thing down," Chip explains. "There was such loud resistance to just someone coming up with some new ideas that, maybe wouldn't work for everyone, but in general may work for many." The opposition to new ideas and outsiders delays progress and creates an unwelcoming environment. That is the opposite of the kind of scene we should be striving to create.

The most direct conflict in the scene often begins in the safest place for a hater to thrive: the internet. "I saw some online slander about our show from [a member of] a band that is pretty big in the Pittsburgh scene," says Nolan. This is a pretty jarring feeling, especially when the hate came from a band you've supported over the last few years. The internet can be an essential tool for a local musician promoting their music, but it can also be a source for people to share their unsolicited negative opinions. Feeling like you are being looked down upon is a common occurrence in the scene that needs to come to an end. It is one thing to receive negative messages from a random person on the internet, but getting them from another band in the scene can destroy and defeat the efforts of valuable community members.

**Radio Hero**

**GhostTown**

**Sky On Fire**

**Days Like This**

**Tears of the Titan**

**Earthquaker**

**Wild Child**

**Pennsylvania**

**One in a Million**

*Ferocious Ghosts setlist*

Unfortunately, no band is exempt from hate comments, regardless of their popularity. According to Mike, Old Neon—who always drew a large crowd—had received very little negative feedback in the past, recalling only “one ‘you suck’ kind of message” on Instagram. However, that changed drastically after the band became involved in performing at drag show events, revealing deeper issues of bigotry within parts of their audience. “The number of bigoted comments we got about the drag show made us realize how important it was that we were doing that.” Mike believes that it was crucial to use Old Neon’s platform to highlight causes and communities they support. “It gives us an obligation to stand up for things that are important to us,” he says.

Deb Cook of Steel Kitty Productions expressed similar frustration with the lack of diversity or fairness in the scene, particularly regarding gender and representation. She pointed out the repetitive nature of these cliques, saying it’s “the same guys promoting the same guys.” Women, LGBTQ+ artists, and people of color navigate the scene differently, experiencing both moments of solidarity and barriers to inclusion.

A committed advocate for diversifying the Pittsburgh music scene, Deb has become a catalyst for that change. “We can't just make safe spaces for our own children,” she said. “We need to make sure that those safe spaces are safe for all children. And I don't think that that is happening.” To help shift the culture, Deb has joined the committee for local festivals to ensure that these underrepresented groups have a fair opportunity to perform, and has organized numerous shows herself to actively foster the inclusive environment the scene needs.

Supporting musicians of all kinds in the scene is just one way we can start to make it a more inclusive environment. Chip Dominick highlights this perfectly. “I'd like to see people being more open to each other, not restricting themselves to doing shows with just their friends,” he says. “Let's not go with what we just know. Let's keep our minds open, keep our ears open, and discover what we don't know already.” The music scene has always been about connections. When we use our voices to amplify one another, we can create a scene that welcomes and inspires.

Community isn’t just about who you know, but about who you are willing to stand beside. Without unity as our shared goal, how can we expect the scene to thrive?

10/31/2025
FUNHOUSE @ MR. SMALLS

OLD NEON

NOBODY'S BURDEN

WDYL

BABY BLUE

BLIZZARD

BETTER SON

WON'T STAY

PEOPLE PLEASER

WASTED

WARMER

BETTER THINGS

*Old Neon setlist*

# GENERATIONS OF MUSIC

The Pittsburgh music scene has been around a lot longer than I have. It is something I have been aware of for my entire life. In fact, it is partially responsible for my life even existing in the first place. My parents may have never gotten together if it wasn't for the music scene. My mom, Sharon, says that I was "born into and through the music scene."

Both of my parents played roles in parts of the local music scene back in the late 80s and 90s, but my family history with the local scene goes back even further than that. Music has been in my DNA for as far back as my family is aware.

My maternal grandmother's father was a guitar player. My grandmother on my dad's side played music with all of her siblings. And my grandfather on my mom's side, Jim Hurray, was a radio DJ for WYEP from 1974-1985. He and my great uncle Fred were co-hosts Youngblood and Mac on WYEP's "Magic Music Machine."

My mom gave me a little history lesson about what my grandfather did. His radio show played mostly 50's and 60's doo-wop music. "A lot of those bands came out of Pittsburgh. If you look at different eras of music and where they came from; LA had hair metal, Seattle had grunge. Well, Pittsburgh had a lot of the doo-wop and 50s sound come out of it."

As according to the Pittsburgh Music History site, "Pittsburgh was one of the centers of Doo Wop and Vocal Group music in the 1950s and early 1960s. An entire industry of Pittsburgh based artists, record labels, DJs, radio stations, and teen dance venues produced and promoted classic Doo Wop and Pop hits that are mainstays of the Doo Wop / Vocal Group revival shows and collectibles releases."

My mom continued, "He and my uncle Fred, every Saturday night for like two or three hours, had a show where they would play the oldies music and then they had people call in and they'd interview them and they were local and also national. He interviewed and met Ray Charles, Chuck Berry, and locally, he was very involved in promoting the Skyliners. They were a Pittsburgh band who became famous."

"He was very involved in the Pittsburgh music scene and lots of people knew who he was. I have fan letters that were sent to him," she told me, showing me envelopes full of letters. Not only does she have letters that were sent to him, but she also has response letters from local bands that *she* wrote fan mail to in her teens and early twenties.

Even though she is not a musician, my mom was still very active as a fan in the music scene in the 90s. Just as I have made it a point to try to go to as many local shows as I can, she did the same when she was my age.

Going through her collection of old flyers, newspaper clippings, local magazines, and photos taken at local shows, I got to get a glimpse into what the music scene (mostly the hair metal part of the scene) was like in the 90s.

She was in Eide's Records when she was 18 and saw a flyer for the local band Raquel and picked it up. "I thought they looked interesting, and they had an address on it. So, I wrote, and the bass player wrote me back, sent me a cassette, and told me that they were recording the Art Institute commercial, inviting me to come to it," my mom says. She went to the filming of the commercial/music video and was instantly hooked on their music.

"I was it was awesome because it was like being able to go see a big national band but in a small venue and you didn't have to feel lost in the crowd," she says. I asked her how often she went to local shows. She said "I started going in high school once in a while. By the time I was 21, every weekend, for sure. Sometimes during the week we'd go to jam nights to check out bands, like on a Wednesday. I would say up to three times a week."

*Flyer for a show in the early 90's*

I had never known about my mom's experience in the music scene when she was in her 20's, but everything she was telling me about herself sounded so similar to what I have been doing over the last two years or so. I thought that it's interesting how similar we are in our perspectives, despite me starting as a musician in the scene, and her being entirely a fan.

"If the band can make you feel like you were seeing a national act, you could go see them for, you know, three dollars, four dollars or whatever. I would rather do that than go to a big concert and be so far away. You learn all their music, and you sing along, and it's just like going to a big show," she told me. Even though she was talking about the hair metal scene from 1990, that quote resonates strongly with me in the rock music scene in 2025.

WE NEED YOUR HELP!
WE WOULD LIKE
ALL OF YOU,
OUR GREAT FANS TO CALL
YOUR LOCAL RADIO STATION
AND REQUEST YOUR
FAVORITE XXX SONG.
...THANKS FOR YOUR SUPPORT...

XXX Merchandise

| | |
|---|---|
| T-SHIRTS | $12.00 |
| POSTERS | $ 3.00 |
| 8 X 10 PHOTO | $ 1.00 |
| VIDEO (PUMP UP THE GAS) | $10.00 |
| LAMINATES | $10.00 |
| RECIEVE $1.00 OFF ALL CLUB SHOWS, JUST SHOW THE DOORMAN YOUR XXX LAMINATE... | |
| COMBO | $20.00 |
| INCLUDES: POSTER • T-SHIRT • LAMINATE | |

XXX

*A page from a newsletter sent out by 90's band, Triple X*

Just the day before talking to her, I had been at the Dormont Music Festival in the front row for Broom, singing along to their songs like *I Wish I Knew*, and *In the Dark,* dancing my heart out as if I had been waiting for my favorite national band to finally come to my city on tour. My mom's experiences in her local scene seem to be shaping up to be almost identical to mine.

Because there seems to be so much similarity, I asked her what the big differences are. "I don't know," she said. "I feel like the only changes is it just seems like it might be harder to get people to come out the shows these days than it was back then." She started showing me printed photographs of her favorite local bands looking for pictures of the crowds. "These places, they would be packed with people."

The biggest difference in that regard goes back to the fact that in this era we have infinitely more methods of entertainment available to us at all times. When my mom was most active as a fan in the scene, there wasn't TikTok or Netflix as options for what to do on a Saturday night, so more people were likely to check out a local band to have something to do.

My mom told me the story of how her and my dad got together. They truly are together because of the

Pittsburgh music scene. My mom said she was friends with a guy in the music scene named Jeff. He had told her about an acoustic show he was playing with one other guy. She went to the show and realized she had met this other guy, Chip, a couple years prior at a mutual friend's graduation party. My dad and Jeff ended up starting a band together called Kick N Grind. My mom continued to go see their band play shows, and eventually my parents got together. They have been together for over 30 years now.

*Kick N Grind*

*Sharon Dominick Photography*

*Flyer for a show in 1992*

# FESTIVALS

One of the key elements that keeps the Pittsburgh music scene alive is festivals. Between large festivals like Millvale Music Festival and North Side Music Festival, and smaller benefit festivals, there is no lack of local music festivals to play.

To name just a handful that I have gotten to play:

- Rock For Life series
- Williams Syndrome Band Bash
- New Castle Music Festival
- Rockin' Roosevelt
- FitzFest

There are too many of them to even list most of, but these are a few annual festivals that I have gotten to play at or attend on more than one occasion. There are some historic festivals such as the Strip District Music Festival and the Rock All Night Tour Festival that unfortunately do not happen anymore.

This chapter poses a big question, even for me as the writer: what qualifies as a festival? It seems like almost any show that has 3 or more bands gets qualified as a festival in the scene. Using the word "festival" in the name of your show started out as a way to hopefully draw in a larger audience, but over time has become overused and is used to describe even the smallest showcases at the smallest venues. Whether your event is three bands in the back of a bar or 300 bands across an entire town, calling it a festival is acceptable.

For the sake of simplicity, I will be talking specifically about festivals that contain 3 or more bands that happen annually.

The community at these festivals is unlike anything else. “The best part is just seeing a bunch of people you never see anywhere else,” says Trish Hosac, who has many different roles in the scene, from managing bands to making interview videos. “You’re always going to make a new friend.”

You never know who you might reconnect with or meet at these festivals, but you can always know you’ll be surrounded by some of the coolest people in town. “Music festivals are a great opportunity to get so many people that may not be involved in the community day to day a chance to hear a plethora of different music,” says Alex Ribeau, vocalist of Never Say Die.

One thing that a lot of bands do to draw traction to their festivals is by having some kind of theme surrounding these festivals. One of the biggest themes for festivals is Halloween. Every year in Pittsburgh, you will never have a lack of Halloween-themed music festivals to go to. In October of 2025, between 2 bands and one solo project, there was at least one local Halloween show I played at or attended every weekend for the entire month. And there are still numerous shows I am disappointed to have missed.

"People always say 'you always have some type of theme around your shows,' whether it's the Heartbreak Ball, or the Halloween show," Cody Kulesa says. "I think that just having a little bit of a gimmick that people can be persuaded to say, 'this isn't just another local band.' There's another little catch, something that just kind of grabs you. And while it's like, don't read a book by its cover, just buy it because of that, people still do that."

This concept is one of the things I have enjoyed a lot about playing with Never Say Die. Most of the festivals we have played are either a benefit show for a good cause, have a really cool theme, or both! The first show that I played with them (not *with* them yet, but The Charge Ups played the same event) was their first annual When We Were Dead Halloween benefit festival.

The second annual When We Were Dead Festival took place one year later in 2025, which I performed with Never Say Die as their official bassist, featured twice as many bands across two stages.

*Never Say Die at When We Were Dead Festival 2025*

*Sharon Dominick Photography*

This show—Cody's brainchild—benefits the Spirit Halloween "Spirit of Children" which goes directly to children's hospitals. The first show raised over $1,000 to be donated, and was an absolute blast to be a part of. Every band that performed that day showed up in costume and put on the show of a lifetime. So many people showed up to dress up in costumes, see some awesome bands, and have a great time.

The show took place again in 2025, with 7 bands and was even more successful than the previous year. The donation to Spirit of Children was over double the first donation, which is an incredible accomplishment. Cody says “As soon as we raised that much money, I knew we were onto something. Big time.” The festival is set to continue annually and will continue to be a growing benefit for children’s hospitals.

The first show I ever played with Never Say Die, filling in on bass, was the Heartbreak Ball, their Valentine’s Day show. Everyone showed up to the show in formal attire, like a high school dance. It seems like one of the easiest ways to get a crowd to show up is to give them a reason to dress up, whether in a costume or a ball gown.

Over the summer, when I officially joined the band, we played more themed and benefit festivals. The first summer show, which I cleverly named Sad Boi Summer, was our summer kickoff show. The next show we played was FitzFest, which is an annual benefit festival raising money and awareness for men's mental health. That festival raised over $7,000 for their cause this year alone. So many people showed up, either to play or to see the bands, and it was an amazing turnout, no matter what stage you were at or what performer you were seeing. The show after that was the second annual Williams Syndrome Band Bash. I had played the first one with Chip & the Charge Ups, and now got to play this event again, as the (official) bassist for Never Say

Die. Getting to support important causes just by playing music, the thing that I love most, feels incredible.

There is never a lack of causes that these festivals support. Band Blast raises funds for the preservation and revitalization of Memorial Park in New Kensington, where the event is held annually. The Rock for Life Concert Series financially supports needy kids in western Pennsylvania who are suffering from life-threatening diseases. There are endless opportunities to go to benefit shows throughout the year, and it is so nice to see bands coming together to raise funds and awareness for good causes.

Every year, Chip & the Charge Ups host a big Festival called Beasts of the Burgh. This is a festival with only 4 bands on it, but at a large venue. Beasts of the Burgh has been hosted at Mr. Small's Theater and

The Club at Stage AE. "The point of it is to bring together four of the hardest-hitting, headline-caliber bands on one stage for one special night only," says Chip. This event draws hundreds of audience members every year and has grown since its birth in 2022. "It's not necessarily the four most popular bands, but the four bands that fit together to create the best experience possible in one night."

Whether your perfect festival means cramming in dozens of bands in a single day, dressing up and diving into a themed world, supporting a cause you care about, or discovering a lineup of heavy-hitting artists who feel like they were made to share a stage, Pittsburgh has it all. There's a festival here for every fan, every mood, and every corner of the scene.

- INTRO/BOTR
- DON'T U
- CALI
- DARK
- HOURGLASS
- CUM TOGETHER
- PANDORA
- UNKNOWN
- IWIK/DRUM SOLO
- FALLING STARS (High Seas)
- BELIEVER
- LTL

BROOM @ Sidequest 11/5/25

*Broom setlist*

# MILLVALE MUSIC FESTIVAL

After 12 hours of dancing my heart out, surrounded by music, sunshine, and many friends, I remembered the point of life again. I always say that Millvale Music Festival is my favorite day of the year, and this year, 2025, was no exception.

*Millvale Music Festival wristband*

My day began quite early for a Saturday gig. I wake up at 9 am to get ready—pick out a badass stage outfit, and do my hair and makeup. We're on the road at 10:30 and arrive in Millvale by 11 am. When we arrive, I have to take a moment's view from the stage, knowing that the blocked-off road will soon be full of fans and locals ready to rock out in the early afternoon. We soundcheck our instruments, and at this point, that was the only thing happening in the whole city. My bass was rumbling every building in a 5-mile radius. This was looking to be extremely promising.

We take the stage at 1, exactly when we were scheduled. I look out into the crowd. Our stage was atop a hill that overlooked Millvale. There are so many people, each playing a different role in the event. There are many familiar faces in the roped-off audience area on Butler Street: friends, family members, fans, and members of other bands. My mom and brother were center stage, right at the front, along with a few friends.

At the table up front on my side of the stage, I see another local band, Broom. The drummer, Carter, is wearing a Chip & the Charge Ups shirt. My friend and coworker Sean—guitarist for the metal band Tiwanaku—shows up with his wife, and the two of them start dancing as we play our original music. I see a guitar student of mine eagerly watching with her family. Alex from Never Say Die is standing with Eric from Rattlebones on the right side of the crowd. Adam and Deb from Aliquid Novi are watching from behind the roped off area on the left side of the stage. Those are just a few of the many familiar faces I saw among the audience. Beyond Butler Street, I can see other bands loading in their equipment, and many employees and volunteers who are working hard to make sure the event runs smoothly and on time.

*Chip & the Charge Ups at Millvale Music Festival 2025*

*Sharon Dominick Photography*

We put on the show of a lifetime, and afterwards, a handful of people lined up at our merch table to take photos, buy merch, and talk to us. It is an indescribable, yet weird feeling, having people be starstruck about talking to me, just a local yinzer. Somehow, that was just the beginning, and the least vibrant of emotions I would be bound to experience.

Now it is time for the fun to begin. I determine that it's time to discover some new local talent, my favorite activity. Moonshine Jasmine takes the same stage I was on at 2 pm, after we had removed our equipment. The singer Megan has such a powerful, bluesy voice that reverberates throughout Butler Street. Next up is Wretched Hearts Club. My friend Luka had told me he had recently joined this band, so I decided to check them out. Their set began at 2:00, but I only caught the last few songs. This band combined so many different genres and styles of music to create something I could never have imagined—but it worked so well. It was like hip-hop music with a rock band.

After their set ended, and scarfing down an order of chips and salsa, I am off to catch one of my all-time favorite locals—PosterChild. I have been a fan of PosterChild from their very first show in 2021, when they were just 16-year-old kids. I had been put on a local showcase at Black Forge II (RIP) with them, and since then, I've been hooked. I have been lucky enough to have shared the stage with them many times, but I know they are destined for greatness much larger than Pittsburgh. Today, they are playing in the brand-new Mr. Small's Sanctuary, the 4th stage added to the Mr. Small's empire. The venue, which is an old church turned into a venue, was beautiful, featuring the original stained glass from when it was a church. It was packed from front to back, making it hard to find a place to stand and have good visibility. Gibson, the frontman, gives a quirky intro before each song. That is a staple of a PosterChild show because he is such an eccentric entertainer and makes every second of the show captivating to watch. They play many tracks off their recently released album, *Vengeance Says*. Every melody Gibson sings sticks in the mind of everyone in the audience, even long after the set is over.

*Gibson Musisko of PosterChild*

*Sharon Dominick Photography*

Finally, all my crew of friends are back together again. They are just drifters in this ocean of local music, but I am on a mission to see many specific bands that I have been dying to check out. I round up the group, and we head over to the Gap Park stage. There are 2 artists that I am dying to see, yet both are playing at the 4:00 hour. The first up is Dizzier. My friend Ben is in this band, as well as an incredibly talented singer, Tupelo. They put on a good show, and Ben's guitar playing blows me away. After a few songs, it is time to run across the entire city of Millvale to catch the next artist I want to see—Aliquid Novi. It is a project of Adam, an artist I met at the open mic, and Deb Cook. After running through traffic, crowds of people, and political marketers on the street, we finally get to Cousin's Lounge for the last 15 minutes of Adam's set. He is playing guitar and singing while Deb is harmonizing with him beautifully. Adam is a very talented songwriter. I only wish that the venue wasn't within earshot of another stage, because it wasn't the easiest to hear Adam, Deb, and a single acoustic guitar over a full rock band playing 2 blocks away.

After their set is over, more friends join the group that I have become in charge of. I now have 6 people who are coming with me to see some of my favorite local artists. The group heads back to the Gap Park stage to see one of the biggest talents in the area right now: Dream the Heavy. The parking lot where this stage is at is packed to the brim with people listening, dancing, and enjoying the music. I make my way to the front of the stage, also meeting up with my dad and his friend Dom. Our group stands on the right side of the stage, directly in front of the bassist, Paul. Dream the Heavy takes not only their musicianship seriously, but evidently every aspect of their performance. The singer, TK, is always in the most unique outfit you could find. His stage presence is so powerful, and he's getting the crowd involved, singing along, snapping, chanting, and other ways to keep the fans engaged. I have had the honor to share the stage with this band twice before, once at the second annual Beasts of the Burgh festival that my band organizes. This fact never fails to amaze me, considering that this band deserves a worldwide following. I had a blast dancing, singing along, and experiencing Dream the Heavy. This made it even more amazing when TK thanked Chip and the Charge Ups for being there from the stage. I am in the front row, fangirling over the musicianship and performance of this band, and they chose to acknowledge and shout out *my band* for being there to support them. If Dream the Heavy were a nationally touring band, I would be waiting out hours before the show to get front row; but instead, they are a local band whom I have had the honor of sharing the stage with.

*Dream the Heavy*

*Sharon Dominick Photography*

After Dream the Heavy, I have 20 minutes to get food and navigate my now 9-person group back to the Butler Street stage to see Rattlebones. We all ended up at the same stage, but not together as a cohesive unit. This is alright with me, because I want to be right at the front of the stage to rock out to the band. Rattlebones puts on a powerful show with incredible rock guitar riffs.

After Rattlebones wraps up their set, we head across the entire town once again to see one of our all-time favorites—Broom! The "venue" they are playing in is the back deck of an axe-throwing place. It is packed already with friends, family, and fans. My crew makes our way to the front. This is my first time seeing them play with their new singer, Noah. As soon as they start playing, I immediately think Noah is the perfect addition to the band. Not only are they talented and put on a good show, but they also pulled out a couple of fun gimmicks. They started passing brooms around the crowd. So many people took turns dancing with, riding on, and fencing with the brooms. The crowd was so engaged and really responded well to the music.

Broom's performance may have been my favorite of the night, just because of how much crowd engagement was happening. They sounded incredible, but on top of that, they made it even more fun for the audience by giving them opportunities to be involved in their set.

*Caleb Beichner of Broom*

*Sharon Dominick Photography*

Like Dream the Heavy, Broom gave a subtle shoutout to Chip & the Charge Ups for being in attendance, referencing our song "Sideways Middle Finger" during their set.

After Broom was done, we took a little break. I bought some Broom merch, talked to the band a bit, had some water, and just sat down and relaxed for about 30 minutes. The only time in the whole day that I would get to do so. But it was over just as soon as it started. We were back on our mission—*my* mission. I knew I wouldn't be able to see every single band that I wanted to see, but I wasn't going to give up on at least getting to see most of them.

We crossed the entire town once again to get to the metal stage. It was now 8 pm, and I had been in Millvale running around for literally 9 hours straight.

The night was not even close to being over yet. We got to the metal stage, and the venue was pretty full! We are here to see Tiwanaku, my friend Sean's band. I see many familiar faces in the venue as his band starts playing. As expected at the metal stage, there are mosh pits and circle pits happening. I get in the pit at one point, but I am not able to keep up with everyone. Tiwanaku slays our ears, and Sean's guitar playing genuinely blows me away. I knew he was a talented guitarist, but this was my first time seeing Tiwanaku play, because they don't typically play in the Pittsburgh area too often.

After the set, I tell Sean what a great job I think he did. My whole crew of people (which has now dwindled down to about 5 of us again) were also all impressed by his playing, as well as the band as a whole.

The next stop on my list is going back to the axe-throwing place to see another long-time favorite, Griffen Handshake. I have played with this band a ton of times over the years, and they were one of the bands on this year's Beasts of the Burgh. I have gotten to know a lot of their songs very well and am so excited to get to see them. They are the last band on my list to see, now at 10 pm. We get to the venue, and I am pleased to see that there is a decent crowd for them as well! They are a 3-piece band, yet you wouldn't know it just by listening to them. I excitedly get to dance and sing along to some of my favorite songs of theirs—*Wings*, *All My Friends Wanna Be Doctors*, and many more bangers. I danced my heart out until I absolutely couldn't anymore. They even gave Chip & the Charge Ups a shoutout for being in attendance. The third one of the day. They ended their set a little after 11 pm. I got to talk to them a bit after their set and told them what a great job they did. We discussed possibly getting to play with them again soon.

*Griffen Handshake*

*Sharon Dominick Photography*

After their set was over, and an incredibly busy 12+ hours, I decided that it was time for me to go home. Nolan and I headed towards the bus stop and reflected on the exciting day we had just experienced.

The last time I got to spend this much time seeing band after band was Four Chord Music Festival. Don't get me wrong, Four Chord is an amazing time, but Millvale will always hold a more special place in my heart. I've been to a handful of big music festivals in my life, including Warped Tour, yet none of these festivals hold a candle to the experience I had at Millvale Music Festival this day.

First of all, Millvale Music Festival is completely free to attend. I got to see at least 10 bands—even more if you consider bands that I stopped to check out just for a song or two. Someone might think that the quality of music at a local festival, such as Millvale, might not be as enjoyable as that of nationally touring bands, but that could not be further from the truth. Every performer that I got to see today was genuinely a musical inspiration. These are world-class songwriters and musicians; only their shows are significantly more accessible.

Millvale Music Festival is where Chip & the Charge Ups began, so it will always be historically significant to us personally and professionally. I was just a 16-year-old girl the first time I had played, and since then have always made an effort to attend the festival, even if I was not performing. Seeing all of your favorite local bands performances can be the most exciting part of the festival, and this year was truly an example of just that.

Three bands had given a shout out to Chip & the Charge Ups from the stage during their performance. This made it very clear to me that it is *so* important to show up for your fellow musicians. It gave me a new perspective. Sure, I was there to support my friends and fellow musicians, but the reason I was there was simply to enjoy amazing music.

At a nationally touring band's show, you will never get a shoutout from the stage just for showing up. There are hundreds to thousands of people who all did the same thing. At a local show, one person's presence makes all the difference. I've thought about this from the perspective of a performer before, but never from the perspective of a fan. Broom, Eric, Alex, Sean, Adam, Deb, and all the other musicians in the crowd at my performance this afternoon meant the absolute *world* to me. However, it had never occurred to me that maybe they were there because they loved my band's music.

Now, looking at it from the audience member's perspective, my mindset had shifted.

My presence at these shows *mattered*. Every person's presence mattered there. Bands supporting each other means something. It is the only way for the scene to grow—for any band or individual musician to grow.

*Chip Dominick*

*Sharon Dominick Photography*

ROAB
VIRGINIA
WITCH BURNER
WAR PIGS
BLACK ELEPHANT
MUD
FAITH
FORTUNATE SON

*Red Coin setlist*

# LOCAL OPENERS

One of the best ways for a local band to get exposure is by opening up for a national or touring band or artist.

I feel very lucky to have gotten the opportunity to open up for some pretty impressive touring artists such as Nita Strauss, Dirty Honey, Liliac, and Dee Snider.

I have heard a lot of people in the scene complain about Drusky Entertainment, but I feel very differently. Many bands and artists seem to feel like they deserve to get paid more than Drusky pays. From my perspective, I know that my band wouldn't have had half of the cool experiences we've had if it wasn't for them. Drusky does almost all of the booking for shows coming through Jergel's, and just about every national show I have been to there has featured a local opener. They are the reason my band got to open up for a lot of the national acts we've opened for. Talking to others in the scene, they also cite Drusky being the promoter that got their bands such gigs.

One of the coolest opportunities for a local band to open for a national act in recent history was the All American Rejects show in August of 2025. Local "grungegaze" band, Eyewash, was asked by the band to open that show. It was a free, surprise pop-up show in the parking lot of Sheetz.

"We were asked to do this not even 5 days before it happened. The show happened on a Friday, and we were notified about it on Monday," says Jake Curran of Eyewash. "The area they gated off for people was about 500 people, but I was told about 2,500 to 3,000 people ended up showing up."

There are very few opportunities for local bands to get to play to a crowd of that caliber. For a band as big as All American Rejects, who typically play stadium shows, to ask a local band to open up for them at this event is a huge win for local musicians.

"The only thing I could think to say was 'how crazy is this?'" Jake continues. "It was a very cool experiences that we couldn't pass up, and we wouldn't trade for anything else. Being able to represent the city of Pittsburgh in that way is pretty special."

*Eyewash performance at Sheetz.*

*Photo credit: Alex Restauri*

Playing these shows gives your band great opportunities to get your music in front of music fans who may not have otherwise had a chance to hear your music. The venues and promoters, such as Jergel's and Drusky, who provide these kinds of opportunities should be celebrated. Though the promoters do take a cut of the money, your band would not have gotten this opportunity without them.

There are tons of bands who are grateful for these experiences, and have gotten even more exciting opportunities because of success at these shows. Midnight Lights told me about opening up for Red Jumpsuit Apparatus. They first opened for them at Preserving for the Four Chord Music Festival Kick-Off Show. And clearly, it paid off for their band as well, considering they had the opportunity to open up for The Red Jumpsuit Apparatus again in 2025. Guitarist,

Tommy, said "We are still so thankful to the promoters for taking a chance on a local band. The whole experience was great—from working with the promoters, venue staff, and other artists to playing our set and catching up with fans at the merch table after, it was a night I'll never forget." Maybe one local opener show doesn't seem like much, but a solid performance at these events can leave a promoter and touring band wanting more.

There have been many examples of this, including my band Chip & the Charge Ups. We have had the opportunity to open for Nita Strauss twice, and Liliac three times. Getting asked to open for the same band a second or third time is even more exciting than the first time, because you know that your performance was perceived to be incredible by the people who matter most when it comes to large shows.

Another positive impact that these shows have are that your band will be viewed as more professional through the eyes of the crowd. Shawn Donahugh Jr. talks about the time his old band, Access Denied, opened for LA Guns. "That show both made a lot of our friends really start to take us more seriously and made us a lot of new fans," he says. Though he was just 15 at the time, he noticed more people in the music scene treating his band with more respect, and more recognition. "The show definitely led to more opportunities, and we took them any chance we got, as long as it was possible for us. It led to us making connections with more local bands, sharing bills with them and making some amazing friendships that still exist today." It is an incredible accomplishment not only for a young band to get a gig opening for a national band, but to also gain recognition as a serious musical endeavor after showing the world their skills.

These shows are all about actively putting your music in front of new ears. It is an opportunity to have a captive audience that has never heard of you before. You have a special opportunity to make yourself and your band known to a wider audience that might not have heard of you otherwise.

Jake Horne told me about how his band, Nephele, opened for Yngwie Malmsteen. "It's not ever an overnight thing making these connections, but putting yourself in the right place, or let alone *more* places, gives you just so much more opportunity to make friends with so many cool people who are doing a lot of cool things!" These opportunities are a great example of why it is important to be in the right place at the right time. So many new ears will get to hear your music, and if you are lucky, the band you are opening for will even come to give your music a listen.

Getting to have a professional show experience that you wouldn't normally get to have is one of the biggest learning experiences a band can have. Amy from Midnight Lights says, "being part of that lineup made us tighten up as a band." A band will learn very fast how to perform and behave in a more professional environment.

From stage performance to fan interactions, to sound checks and networking, the experience will be significantly more impactful and insightful than any experience at your average bar gig. Megan from Moonshine Jasmine says, "we had chances to see how the true pros handle a live show. We got to experience what a real production crew feels like. It gave us confidence to move through the ‘shitty’ gigs. It helped us push ourselves to polish our sets.”

Lastly, these gigs do often pay significantly more than a typical local show, and they’re easier to promote since fans are eager to see the headlining band. Bands can sell tickets to both their supporters, and fans of the touring act, who may never otherwise attend a local show. Beyond just financial benefit, these opportunities can be game-changing for a band’s growth. These experiences improving stage presence, learning professional production, and connecting with new fans can shape a band’s trajectory in major ways.

- **Mr. Unknown**

---

- **Larger Than Life**
- **I'm a Believer**

---

- **(California)**
- **(Sweet Home Alabama)**
- **Paranoid**

---

- **I Wish I Knew**

---

- **Kids In America**

*Broom setlist*

# SUBSCENES

There is one major flaw in the community that has been made obvious through this research, and it is something that has shown up recently. This could be due to venues closing, oversaturation of bands, too many options for entertainment, or a combination of other factors. That issue is this: *there are no longer venues you can go to every weekend to see a different band of the same subscene.*

Just a few years ago, one would be able to walk into the 31st Street Pub, Howlers, Black Forge, or any venue of their preference and see a show from a band in the same style as the band that was there the previous weekend. Now, most venues do not stick to booking certain types of bands. This can be cool for people who live near a venue and are open to any genre of music, but this can be a big concern when trying to get people to come to shows.

One could show up at the 31st Street Pub on a random Saturday and be sure to see a hard rock band with killer original music. One could walk into Black Forge II on a Saturday and know that they would get to hear indie music made by talented college students and be sure to be surrounded by a vibrant under 21 community.

These particular venues had a built-in crowd: people who would show up at the venue every Saturday night because they knew they would be getting top-tier entertainment in their preferred style of music regardless of which bands were being booked that weekend. Unfortunately, now, all these venues are closed, and the city is very limited on small to medium capacity venues.

If you were to walk into Mr. Small's Funhouse, the Mr. Roboto Project, or Bottlerocket, there is no guarantee of what kind of music that you would hear.

This is not an inherently bad thing. There are so many more shows being curated featuring musicians of all genres, and it provides incredible opportunities for networking, and collaborating with musicians you may have never met otherwise. Those kinds of events can actually help destroy some of the problems with exclusivity and gatekeeping in the scene. However, the problem lies in the lack of community building opportunities within specific genres and venues.

This doesn't mean that there aren't still many opportunities to build that kind of community. It just means that it will require more flexibility, promotion, and willingness to check out new venues.

# The 10 biggest local music stories of 2021

Ben Braun/Post-Gazette

Chip Dominick of Chip & The Charge Up's plays at the Millvale Music Festival in August.

mise of the Rex Theater, Cattivo and Brillobox, the survivors got help, from the top and up to the grassroots.

In an effort to save Moondog's, musicians put together a virtual concert in March to raise more than $65,000 for the long-running Blawnox blues club.

In January, Rocky Lamonde, bassist for The Borstal Boys and producer at The Vault, launched the virtual SOS (Save Our Stages) Live Series, featuring garage and punk bands playing from Pianos 'N Stuff, and he followed with a second series in April featuring jazz, blues and singer-songwriters. It raised a few thousand dollars and, more importantly, awareness.

"We were trying to raise money," Lamonde said, "but I think our goal was more about spreading the word of the SOS national campaign and awareness so that the bill could be passed and people can contact their legislators to get money in the hands of the clubs."

Those U.S. Small Business Administration's Shuttered Venue Operators Grants, the result of that bill, were frustratingly slow in the launch, but the money finally began to drop in July with millions of dollars spread between organizations such as the Pittsburgh Cultural Trust and Pittsburgh Symphony Orchestra to clubs like The Roxian, Mr. Smalls and Spirit.

**3. Hello, AO!**

Given the perils of the pandemic on people's health and wealth, The Allegheny Overlook was a perfect escape.

The pop-up venue, sitting on a colorful sidewalk mural by Janel Young, appeared on the AO along Fort Duquesne Boulevard for the Three Rivers Arts Festival, and then continued on through the summer thanks to Pittsburgh Downtown Partnership.

It kept Downtown lively and bustling on weekend nights with performances by Jim Donovan & Sun King Warriors, The Houserockers, Bindley Hardware Co., Jordan Montgomery and many others. It also became a paid venue for Fitz & The Tantrums when the show was moved from the drive-in theater.

If you hit it just right, you could see a band followed by a post-game Skyblast from the Pirates.

**4. Our country superstars**

There was no slowing down in 2021 for

SEE **MUSIC**, PAGE WE-11

*Newspaper article from Pittsburgh Post Gazette*

There are so many different subscenes in the overarching Pittsburgh music scene. The most prominent one from my perspective is the rock scene, but there are different scenes within that as well.

There are a handful of bands in a much more popular rock subscene, for example: Gene the Werewolf, The Hawkeyes, Tiny Wars, and of course,

The Clarks. These are bands that often record in some of the best studios with the best producers, get regular airplay on WDVE, and always get to play the big stages at local festivals. Their musical greatness is undeniable, even to people who aren't interested in local music. These bands don't play shows as often as many bands do, but when they have performances, the venues are packed to the brim.

There are a ton of amazing rock bands in the scene that, despite not always getting the biggest opportunities, still get regular gigs at big venues. These are the hundreds, if not thousands, of bands that come from all over the greater Pittsburgh area.

Chip Dominick has been organizing the Beasts of the Burgh music festival since 2022 and gives bands in this subscene the opportunity to play at legendary Pittsburgh venues, like Mr. Small's Theatre and Stage

AE's "Club at Stage AE." He says, "the artists that we've had have come from all corners of the Pittsburgh music scene and showcase the talent that we have here. I think it introduces people to bands that they may never have heard of before and pleasantly surprises them." He strives to get new bands on the lineup every year, and to one day grow the event to be able to feature even more bands. If this is the scene you are involved in, you will never lack new bands to discover and support.

Within the rock music scene, there are many subgenres, but there are opportunities for cross-pollination in these scenes. However, it tends to be the same bands playing with the same bands most of the time. Pop-punk bands only play with other pop-punk bands. Metal bands only play with other metal bands. Some bands only book shows with their friends' bands. There is nothing inherently wrong about show curation featuring similar artists, but there are tons of opportunities for new combinations just waiting to happen.

Occasionally, you will see a lineup with metalcore bands like Ire and Star Viper playing the same show as an alt-rock band with funk roots like Dream the Heavy. Sometimes you will see a blues punk band like Rebel Revolver playing with an indie synth band like Jaaye. These opportunities don't happen every weekend.

Regardless of whether these rock bands are playing with bands of other styles, or sticking to what they know, there is always collaboration on the shows that are being booked.

There are so many resources for the bands in the rock corner of the scene. Local radio stations like 97.7 the Rock Station consistently play local rock bands.

102.5 WDVE has the Homegrown Show which features local rock music. Even 105.9 The X does a local listen featuring rock bands who are putting out hard-hitting music. The local music festivals like Millvale and North Side Music Festivals are great resources for this massive rock scene as a whole, as well as many other genres.

The country music scene, on the other hand, tends to lack collaborative shows. However, despite lack of collaborations on shows or events, the country music scene seems to be a tight-knit community as well. "Everybody at one point or another ends up knowing each other or talking or becoming friends," says Nathan King. According to Nathan, the community often collaborates and supports one another with studio work: "I've had a lot of pretty well-known people work on music for me. If I ask, 'Hey, do you know someone who can play this instrument?' they'll say, 'Oh yeah, give this guy a call,' and it turns out he plays for one of the top five artists in the world—and then that person actually gets back to you." Collaborations within the community are one of the factors that brings musicians together for the greater good of the scene.

*Maleena & Nolan Allen at Mr. Roboto Project*

*Sharon Dominick Photography*

Though there are many cool big opportunities such as festivals and opening for national acts, or working with well-known musicians, Pittsburgh also has a thriving DIY scene. From DIY venues like the Mr. Roboto Project, to house shows and basement shows, there is a rich underground culture.

"It's the most DIY of all DIY things," says Zachk Cain of Catatoneya. Zachk was a part of Steel City Death Club for years prior to the pandemic, which was a media collective to create shows and promotional content for the bands in this scene. "It was pitched to me kind of like having ambitions of being a record label, but really just being a collective for people who enjoy hanging and making music to have an excuse to do so more." During this era, this subscene of music was full of new content all the time. "They were churning out a live video every couple of weeks, had a full website, putting on events as much as fun was definitely prioritized there was a lot of ambition there," he says.

A huge staple of the DIY scene is house shows. The average music fan might not have high expectations for these kinds of events, but they are always packed, wall to wall in the basements of old Pittsburgh city houses. "You can't beat a damp, crowded, smelly, beer-soaked basement," says Zachk. "It's in a constant state of change," he adds, "the people that run them are just college kids. When they graduate or move on to whatever else in their lives, the venues often just disappear."

Despite having basements full of dozens if not hundreds of college kids drinking beer and starting mosh pits, the community at these events are very positive and uplifting. You can often find the most dedicated fans, who are not musicians, just at the shows to enjoy the local scene.

If sweaty basement punk shows aren't your vibe, there are many more outlets for acoustic music. One of the subscenes that I have especially loved being a part of is the AcoustiCafe singer-songwriter community. The open mic happens every Monday at Mr. Small's Funhouse. There are always a mix of regular attenders and newcomers to this event no matter when you decide to come.

Though the event is just an open mic on Mondays, the community built at this event stretches far beyond a once-per-week occurrence. This scene is very collaborative. Artists who attend often ask other musicians to play on their songs during open mic, and even at their shows. There is always a house band who can learn an artist's song on the spot to be able to perform alongside them and give their performance the full-band feel. Many of these artists perform shows together.

Mr. Small's Café hosts the AcoustiCafe songwriter series, where different artists who regularly perform at the open mic can perform a full set. Additionally, the community comes together to perform at larger events. At the Fourth of July festival in downtown Pittsburgh, this community got the headlining slot on the Main Stage. Called "Mr. Small's Presents 90's Summer Jam." Different artists who regularly perform at the open mic got the opportunity to sing covers of 90's rock and alternative songs with a version of the AcoustiCafe house band. They also often host other 80's or 90's themed events at Mr. Smalls. This community also often hosts open mic opportunities on big stages at major local festivals like Millvale Days.

*Deb Cook of Steel Kitty Productions & Aliquid Novi*

*Sharon Dominick Photography*

As for jazz music in Pittsburgh, there are always opportunities for musicians at restaurants like Con Alma, or at local wineries. Matthew Cross, the drummer of Lisa Jay & the TriO says that his band, though they mostly play jazz, switch up their set depending on the venue. "We have different arrangements of the same song to play at different venues," he says. The group often plays in high-end restaurants, which Matthew enjoys, but he wishes there were more outlets for jazz bands in Pittsburgh. "I would love a bunch of different places for the jazz scene," says Matthew, "being able to go to a club where people want to go and sit down and listen to some good jazz standards or original music."

Many artists in the rap scene describe it as "competitive." Between the drive of all the musicians to make it to the top, and factors such as rap battles, there are always motivating factors for these artists to make themselves known. One artist, Eldoon, says "I started in the scene freestyling. That in itself isn't necessarily competitive. It can be, but I always looked at it as just good fun. However, I have been in battles where money is on the line." This is something that differs from many other subscenes in Pittsburgh, as rap battles and competitions as a core part of this scene. While there are different battles of the bands, they are not staples in these other communities. “Sometimes, when you see a flyer with open slots, it's definitely better to just nab the spot while you can. Because other artists are equally as hungry to perform as you. And your opportunity will be gone in an instant if you aren't careful,” Eldoon says.

One difference about the rap scene is that there does seem to be a hub developing for these artists at The Forge Urban Winery. Though it is not as frequent as every weekend, TJC Presents is often hosting rap shows and festivals at this venue multiple times per month.

KGVSUNIVERSE notes that in the rap scene, “people have their dedicated groups, and don’t like to work amongst other groups.” Being a somewhat recent transplant to Pittsburgh just a few years ago, it took a while to find his place in the scene. “Over time, it has only gotten easier, as more people have come forward to support.” When describing the part of the scene he is involved in, he said he could sum it up in one word: diverse.

The rap and hip-hop scene can also be more collaborative than other genres, allowing for events with dozens of performers on the same bill, and using the performances to hype up or perform with other artists.

There are communities of musicians in the Pittsburgh scene that many may not even be aware of, like classical music. Jim Rodgers, the principal bassoonist for the Pittsburgh Symphony Orchestra says “it's the biggest classical organization in town. That's definitely its hallmark. I suppose just from an intrinsic standpoint, it has the biggest budget. And it's also mostly classical but, we branch off into different genres."

Though many people think of a symphony as strictly classical music, the PSO has done performances of many genres, covering music from The Beatles to Pink Floyd, to Led Zeppelin, and to movie soundtracks. Jim says that while the PSO differs in many ways, music is what connects every part of the scene together. "What you do and what we do are connected, because we make music," he states. One incredible collaboration that the Symphony did was with rapper Frzy. To combine a rapper with a full symphony is an incredible creative endeavor.

Frzy recalls, "We had so many people telling us that we couldn't do it. We dealt with so much racism, and we dealt with so much, 'this doesn't happen, we don't do this here.'" Combining these two genres was a major risk for everyone involved, but it ultimately paid off in the long run.

"We were gonna make it a clean show because they were so worried about their subscribers. Maybe like a day or two before the show, they said, 'Do what you want,'" Frzy says. "For a lot of people, hearing somebody yell, 'fuck,' or 'put your hands up,' was crazy for them. But seeing everybody's response—we had a party. I built a relationship with them," he continues. "I've given Pittsburgh so much. To me that was Pittsburgh saying, 'I love you too.'"

Jim Rodgers had an equally positive experience being on the symphony side of the performance. "I was definitely a fanboy," he admits. Open-minded and creatively adventurous, Jim expresses so much excitement about performing any kind of music, even if other symphony members question it. "I thought it was wonderful," he says. "It did shock a few people because he dropped a lot of F-bombs all over the place. People asked, 'should we really be supporting this?' Well, you can decide."

Jim expressed deep gratitude for performing with Frzy. "The thing that impressed me just so much was his artistry, his creativity, and how he had honed his craft to such a perfection." Jim admires Frzy's "presence, his magnetism, and his genuine love for what he was doing, and that we got to share it."

These kinds of experiences go to show that despite there being many different subscenes, the Pittsburgh community can function together in many different combinations.

Regardless of which subscene you choose to get involved in, a shared love for music and community unites everyone as one big family. "More artists are coming together, no matter the differences they've had in the past," says KGVSUNIVERSE. "Feeling how alive the live music scene is—from rock, country, rap, even jazz—it's definitely remarkable to experience."

*Brad Yoder, Amy Mmhmm, Deb Cook*

*Sharon Dominick Photography*

September 18, 2025 - Jergel's - Warrendale, PA

**Paying Back the Devil**

-------------------------------(Maleena intros next song, Chip changes guitar)

**Mr. Brightside**

**Welcome to the Neighborhood**

**What's My Age Again**

------------------------------------ (Chip intros next song)

**Not Van Halen's Jump**

**I'm Not Okay**

**Sideways Middle Finger**

**Holiday**

------------------------------------ (Nolan intros next song)

**Missing Socks**

**Glory**

**Face Down**

**Addicted (big ending)**

------------------------------------ (Maleena intros next song, Chip changes guitars)

**King for a Day**

**Where I Fit In**

**Ocean Avenue**

------------------------------------ (Nolan intros next song, Maleena changes guitars)

**Maleena Made Us**

**The Tide Is High**

------------------------------------ (Chip intros next song)

**The Ol' Two-Niner**

*Chip & the Charge Ups setlist*

# YOUTH IN THE SCENE

When I was 15 years old, I started booking my own shows. Almost ten years later, this amazes me. It is already difficult enough speaking to a teenager as an adult, trying to decipher the new gen-alpha slang words, so the fact that any venues took chance and trusted me to single-handedly run an event is amazing.

I had been playing shows with For Those About to Rock Academy, School of Rock, and acoustic gigs with my dad leading up to this point and had just started my solo musical career. It was 2017, and there were still so many local venues open for musicians to play at. In May of 2017, I played my first solo show at the legendary Hambone's. This was an acoustic show that my dad was hosting, called Turn Down To Ten Fest. My dad, Chris Callen, and Doug Carnahan were each playing an acoustic set. They needed an artist to open up the show, and somehow, I was deemed good enough to be that person. This was huge for me, considering I had *just* learned how to play guitar.

At 15 years old, I had been going through my first-ever heartbreak, and I turned to songwriting to cope. I had an electric guitar, but I wanted an acoustic so that I could play solo acoustic shows, just like Turn Down to Ten Fest. My dad had me do a bunch of chores: vacuuming the whole house, washing his car, and other similar tasks. Between the chores I did and the money I had saved up, I had enough that could get my own acoustic guitar. My dad took me to Guitar Center to pick one out, and Tony Willoe was there to be the salesperson that I needed. Tony had helped me when picking out many instruments in my past: my first-ever bass, my acoustic bass that I had picked up to play on acoustic shows with my dad, and now my first acoustic guitar. I ended up getting the Yamaha FSX800C, which helped me write hundreds of songs.

After I got that Yamaha acoustic, I wasted no time. I got the guitar in April of 2017, and immediately, I wrote my first *real* song, "Flashbacks," which ended up being released on my debut album, over 3 years later. Playing my first gig at Hambone's in May of 2017 was both exciting and terrifying. At 15 years old, you don't realize the reality of the difficulties of being a musician. For all I knew, this show could be my big break. Of course, it wasn't. But it was the debut of a long musical career that I am incredibly proud of. That gig, though historically insignificant, was the first of many things that motivated me, and sparked my passion for the local scene and being a part of it.

I got another gig in June of 2017, at Joe's Crab Shack. When you are just getting started in the music scene (and even after you become a seasoned veteran, to an extent), a gig is a gig, and you take every opportunity you can get. And by that time, I was already making moves to bigger, greater things…

I booked my own gig. It was set to be on July 5th, 2017. It was a Monday, but it was summer, and I was too young to have a job. I had emailed Black Forge Coffee House, the best venue for under-21 performers, and to my excitement, they agreed to let me host this show.

As an adult who worked at a concert venue, I do not know who approved this show or why they trusted a 15-year-old kid to book a profitable event, but I am endlessly grateful that they did.

I got to work right away. My first step was to find other performers for this event. I wanted to make a special opportunity for youth musicians just starting their journeys (a goal that I have continued to work towards through my various jobs in music education.) The first person I asked was my friend Emily. She was someone I had met through School of Rock and became friends with very quickly. Next, I asked my friend Ricky, who sat next to me in the viola section of our high school's orchestra. The third person I asked was my friend Tanner and his band. I had met him because his mom and my dad had been in a band together previously. All 3 acts said yes, and that it would be their first *real* show they were playing, despite all having other performance outlets.

music

**Maleena Dominick, 18, steps away from the Charge-Ups with debut album**

By Scott Mervis
Pittsburgh Post-Gazette

Maleena Dominick releases her debut album "Bruises to Prove It."

Sharon Dominick

When you ask an 18-year-old about her biggest music inspirations, you don't expect her to name-check an artist who doesn't have a major hit and has done some of his most high-profile work as a producer.

"I never try to replicate anything that anyone has done before," says Maleena Dominick, "but one of my favorite songwriters and my biggest inspiration is Butch Walker. I'm a big fan of real, raw emotions in songs and that's something I try to do with my songs."

Walker's influence can be heard in Chip and the Charge-Ups, a Pittsburgh power-pop band fronted by her father, Chip Dominick, in which she plays bass and sings backup vocals.

On Friday, Maleena veers off with her first solo record, "Bruises to Prove It," a six-song collection of pop-rock topped with her airy vocals, honed as a member of the Pittsburgh Youth Chorus.

Starting with recorder and viola in school, Dominick set out to become a bass player when she was 10.

"At that time, I knew I couldn't play guitar," she says. "It wasn't something that was easy for me. I tried before. So, me and my dad went to The Guitar Center and I said, 'Hey, that doesn't have as many strings, maybe I could play that one.' I thought it would be easier for me to play, and it was."

Within four or five years, she was able to play guitar as well, and when she was 16, she formulated an ambitious project.

"I decided that I wanted to start taking it seriously, so I set up this project that by 2020 I wanted to put an album out and I would write 20 songs and would choose the six best to put on the album."

Along with playing in the Charge-Ups, that's what she did. She wrote on guitar and piano and made demos on ProTools while saving money for five days of studio time last summer at Innovation Studios.

"My dad helped out with the guitar riffs and we have a friend from church, Ed [Gourley], who helped out with the drums. I gave them some direction of what I wanted to do with the songs and we all put it together and it turned out really good."

One song, "I Can't Find You," was recorded the summer before that Real Life Music Camp, the program run by Rusted Root's Liz Berlin.

The title, "Bruises to Prove It," came during a discussion with her photographer mom, Sharon.

"It came up and it just kind of clicked," she says. "This is what I've been working for the past two years and I have the bruises to prove it. When I started this, there was a feeling of, 'You're 16. There's no way you're going to be able to pull off a two-year project.' But this was all self-motivated and self-created."

Leading up to the release, Dominick, who will study at music tech at Duquesne University in the fall, won the Hall of Personal Expression (H.O.P.E.) contest, which is sponsored by Robbie's Hope Foundation — a Colorado-based nonprofit with the mission to stop the teenage suicide epidemic — for the single "Don't Forget Me."

She will perform songs from the album on release day, Friday at 7 p.m. on her Instagram and Facebook pages.

*Article from Pittsburgh Post Gazette by Scott Mervis*

Next, I had to start advertising. I designed flyers, social media posts, and even numbered tickets to be printed out. I even named the event: Monday Night Music Mayhem.

I prepared every single day for this event. That meant practicing my setlist, convincing my friends to get their parents to drive them to the venue, posting every day, and selling tickets. By the time the day came,

I was sufficiently prepared for the greatest event of all time.

Show day came and I arrived at the venue ready to be a professional promoter and run the show better than any other band that had ever played at Black Forge Coffee House ever has. While that probably didn't happen, the show ended up being a major success. If the event wasn't sold out, it was damn close, because the place was packed. Wall to wall, front to back, there were people ready to support and listen to the future of local music.

This day gave me so much hope for a bright future ahead of me. I had gotten an opportunity, not only for myself, but also to help out several other young musicians getting started in the music scene.

*Performers from Monday Night Music Mayhem, 2017*

*Sharon Dominick Photography*

Black Forge Coffee House. The hub for young musicians, for a very brief period. The place where so many under-21 bands got their first opportunities.

The first Black Forge location in Allentown was great, but Black Forge II in McKees Rocks took the cake when it came to factors like venue size and crowd draw. At Black Forge II, there was always a built-in crowd of 40+ college students every weekend.

John Noll, who ran sound at Black Forge, says the venue was “a place to learn, and a place to fuck up without judgement. Kids should have more options than just playing in bars and having to be in those environments. They aren’t the type of place that can nurture and help a young performer’s mind and body.”

Black Forge was the starting place for many young bands in the scene, and where they really learned to grow as a performer and songwriter. The atmosphere was more inspiring than any other venue, and the people who showed up were the most enthusiastic crowd a young band could ever imagine.

The one “promoter” who organized these shows was a polarizing figure. Despite being shady, taking money from teenagers, and never attending any of the shows he hosted, the scene that was born during the era he was active was magical. Almost all of the shows that I went to and/or played at Black Forge II were organized by this person. Though I never met this person, I did get to meet so many people who would continue to be a part of the music scene in big and impactful ways.

This community was so positive and uplifting. John says, "all the bands always stayed to support, and even amongst many gigs full of confusion, nobody ever fought with each other or made the show bad behind the scenes." Truly, every band and artist who played at this venue came in with an open mind and a kind heart. Everyone who played there was truly in it for the love of making music. John continues, "there was a fostered kindness that made each other less nervous and more at home on stage, as well as behind the scenes. A community cannot continue without those types of foundations leading them."

The first show I played at Black Forge II was in August of 2021. It was just a solo acoustic performance from me, but the other artists on the lineup were full bands. Two of the other bands that played that day were Mellowscape and Griffen Handshake, who I have continued to play shows with, and have attended their shows.

After that first show, I was inspired to play my own original music with a full band. Once I had the Music by Maleena Band, I got a regular gig at Black Forge. I played there at least once per month from mid-2021 to mid-2022. Around that time, the gigs slowed down as both Black Forge locations were preparing to close their doors. John says that what he wishes everyone would remember about the venue is it being a positive part of their lives. "Whether it was iced coffee in the summer with friends, or a place to go to scream your lungs out, we had your back. I hope people remember their first dates, botched setlists, laughing in the parking lot, and being reckless in the name of rock 'n roll."

An unfortunate loss, but the community that was born from this venue remains strong. Many bands I got the chance to play with at Black Forge still attend my shows, and I attend theirs, if not playing shows together at other venues. To name a few of the other bands that were a major part of this scene: PosterChild, Main Street Detour, Herald's Goose, Bad Judgement, and I Swallow Ghosts.

| | |
|---|---|
| For the Love of Everything Beautiful | Am / A |
| I Can't Find You | Eb |
| Nowhere to Hide | C |
| Change | E |
| Do I Even Make a Difference | C |
| Homesick | A |
| Growing Up | C |
| Strong Enough to Break | Bb |
| On the Run | E |
| Not that Kinda Love Song | F |
| Red Flags | Eb |
| Burn it Down | C |
| Reprise | A |

*Maleena setlist*

By the time I was 16, I was ready to be in a band. After joining or creating a few projects that inevitably failed, I was starting to feel hopeless. No one I met had the same drive and motivation that I had, and I was not willing to settle for less.

Around this time, my dad had been trying to form a band as well. He brought many people into our house to jam with or audition for his band. Eventually, he found a guitarist and a drummer, but was struggling to find a bassist. He had asked me to fill in for practice a few times, and I kept showing up and learning his songs. Eventually, he got a gig at Millvale Music Festival in 2018. I played with them, and from that day forward, I was the official bassist of Chip & the Charge Ups.

Though I am now an adult, I still want to see opportunities for young people to get into the music scene. I have been involved in teaching music lessons for a few years now. In 2024, I started organizing jam nights for my students at the studio where I teach. I had dozens of students coming and having the greatest time getting to finally play with other students who were passionate about music.

Once all of the students were comfortable playing with each other, I knew it was time to host an event. I booked a date at Mr. Small's Funhouse for my students to have a showcase. About 20 students ranging in age from about 7 to 17 performed at this event. When the day of the show came, the venue was packed from wall to wall. Many friends and family members showed up to support these students. Some students were nervous, others were excited. Regardless, everyone had a great time and put on the best show. Not only was I incredibly proud of all of these students, but they were all proud of themselves. Dozens of young kids and teenagers left the venue that day feeling a newfound sense of accomplishment and an even brighter passion for the music they had been making.

One of the biggest challenges facing the young people in the music scene is the lack of places to perform, especially after the unfortunate loss of both Black Forge locations. “I’ve always thought that the music scene could use more all-ages venues,” says Chip Dominick. “It’s important if we always want to have a strong, sustainable music scene to make sure that culturally, we have our young people coming into the music scene.”

Though there are few places to play, there are certainly people in the scene working hard to create these opportunities for young people. Liz Berlin is a great example. She currently runs a program called We Rock Workshop which is a music program for kids who have been or are currently in the foster care system. In the past she has run Real Life Music camp as well which is a program for young kids looking to get involved in the music industry.

Despite not being many, there are still opportunities for young people to get involved in the scene. Whether it is through School of Rock, the youth stage at Millvale Music Festival, or showing up at AcoustiCafe open mic, there are still chances for these young voices to be heard.

Hopefully, opportunities for the under-21 crowd will become more accessible in the future. The youth of the scene now are the future of the scene entirely. Who will be the guiding voice that will lead this generation to greatness?

NSD - WSBB - 8/2/25

Hearts Burst into Flames
Animal I Have Become
Artist/Ambulance
Change
My Curse

C G C F

Changes TUNE (cass + mike)

Someday
Happy Life → F#

DADG

Fall From Me - CDE
The Mirror - C A♭ G

EADG

Ohio is for Joey

Thats What You Get #9 11
One Step

C# G# C# F#

*Never Say Die setlist*

# UNDERREPRESENTED VOICES

Excitement coursed through my veins as I looked out from the vocal booth while singing the lyrics to my original song, *I Can't Find You*. I could not believe that my first experience recording a song I wrote was at the same studio many of my musical heroes had been in before. I had been writing songs, intending to release an album, for about a year at this point in 2019. Because of the Pittsburgh legend, Liz Berlin of Rusted Root, I was taking my first step towards doing so. Liz has done so much for the young and underrepresented voices in the scene, providing aspiring musicians with a professional recording and performance opportunity at her Real Life Music Camp. I leave the vocal booth and walk into the control room. "I came up with a harmony to add," Liz says. I could not believe that someone as talented and successful as her wanted to help me, a 17-year-old girl with minimal songwriting experience. I look around the room to see the people I had just met. There were so many people of different backgrounds, but here we all are together, getting to collaborate and support each other. Everyone was speaking up and pitching new ideas to one another about the songs we had all written. Being able to collaborate with open-minded and supportive peers to create something I am so proud of is a core memory that I will treasure for the rest of my life.

*Real Life Music Camp 2019*

*Sharon Dominick Photography*

Real Life Music Camp is a perfect example of how we can work to make the music scene a better place for everyone involved. It is so important to be able to support all of the people in the music scene, not just the ones who have easy access to it, or the ones who are already well established.

It is incredibly important to not only work with the people that you know and are friends with, but also to give opportunities to people who have different backgrounds. Frzy, a prominent figure in the hip-hop scene, shares a valuable experience about humility and collaboration. Reflecting on his New Year's performance in Pittsburgh, he shared how he stepped aside during his set to highlight fellow artist, Bird. "I could have just stood on stage and hyped her," he said, "but I took that opportunity to walk off stage and get some water, because I wanted her to have that moment on stage by herself to just rock—and she killed it." His choice to uplift another artist in a high-profile moment demonstrates the importance of sharing the spotlight and using your platform to elevate others. True leadership in music doesn't come from dominating the stage, it comes from sharing the spotlight and creating opportunities for *everyone*.

Unfortunately, opportunities don't come quite as easily to everyone in the scene. Real Life Music Camp is where I first met Deb Cook. At the time, I was just a teenager. She was a mentor, and a huge help to me breaking into the scene, and as I have gotten older, she has transformed into a great friend as well. I wouldn't have found my place in the scene as easily as I did without her guidance, and she is always striving to provide that kind of support for others in the scene.

"I very quickly learned that women, people of color, and people on the LGBTQ+ spectrum don't really have the same opportunities as straight white men," she said. "So, I shifted my focus to helping the underrepresented voices here on Pittsburgh." Deb has organized so many shows that feature amazing, talented people.

"I try to bring new people into the music scene, and I try to build them up," Deb says. She hosts AcoustiCafe every November and not only has an all-female house band, but she's also always bringing new young musicians into that scene. "I do what I can with what I have, and when I do that, I bring new voices," she says.

"It's really important that we find spaces for people who don't drink, for people who are kids, for people who maybe don't feel safe in a predominantly male situation," says Deb. She notes that the crowd at the open mic is predominantly men, and has made it a priority to bring more women into that environment. I had never heard of the open mic until Deb invited me to come play with her one Monday several years ago, when I was 20. Since then, I have watched her consistently open doors and serve as a welcoming and guiding force for new people to come and participate in this incredible weekly event.

"Our guys need to step up," she adds. "It's not just about when you remember, or 'allowing' girls in that space, but it's actively choosing them. We need to actively be putting new people in those positions. It's important to not just find opportunities for people but create them."

Mike McInnes of Old Neon shares a similar mindset about inclusivity. "Four of us are straight white guys," he says. "We have a louder voice, and we need to fucking use it."

Deb's words capture the heart of what real inclusivity looks like: "When you are doing something, bring someone else with you." Change doesn't always come from sweeping initiatives but often starts with one person choosing to make room for another. If we want underrepresented voices to thrive, we all have a role to play in amplifying them, encouraging them, and making sure they're part of the spotlight.

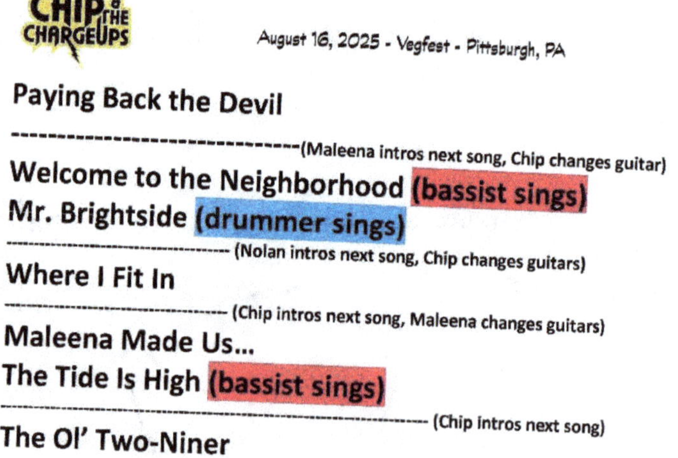
CHIP & THE CHARGEUPS

August 16, 2025 - Vegfest - Pittsburgh, PA

Paying Back the Devil

-----------------------------(Maleena intros next song, Chip changes guitar)

Welcome to the Neighborhood (bassist sings)

Mr. Brightside (drummer sings)

----------------------------- (Nolan intros next song, Chip changes guitars)

Where I Fit In

----------------------------- (Chip intros next song, Maleena changes guitars)

Maleena Made Us...

The Tide Is High (bassist sings)

----------------------------- (Chip intros next song)

The Ol' Two-Niner

*Chip & the Charge Ups setlist*

# WHY THESE CONNECTIONS (SHOULD) MATTER

I often discuss the Pittsburgh music scene with my friends and family, and there is one main point that I always emphasize as a persuasive factor for why people should support it. You can spend $5 to $10 to see the most talented musicians and songwriters you've ever seen, *and* you can talk to them and befriend them after the show. In a society full of parasocial relationships, these kinds of connections are more important than ever. Not to mention that some of these musicians may become (or already are) world-class musicians. Every band you've ever loved started as a local band at one point.

"Local music is the best value for your entertainment dollar," says Utah Burgess of Shady Lady Productions. "The talent is on par with anything else you're going to spend way more money on."

It always blows my mind when I see people spending hundreds of dollars on concert tickets to sit a thousand yards away from the stage for a musician who will never know that they exist yet refuse to pay $5 to see their equally talented friends and family from the front row in a small club.

**That is what makes the people who do even more special.**

I look at the text that pops up on my phone screen from my mom. It is a screenshot of an Instagram story. "Filling in tonight with @zackwiesinger at @poetrylounge in Millvale. 8 pm." Posted by Anthony

Sonetti, drummer of Badflower. Badflower is one of my favorite bands of all time. They are a nationally touring band based in LA, but 2 of the members of the band live in Pittsburgh and are fairly active in the area.

"Omg!" I reply.

"That place looks so tiny!" my mom sent back.

Anthony, despite being in a band that tours the entire globe, being direct support for major bands like Three Days Grace and 311, is still active in the local music scene when he is not touring. My mom, who is a professional photographer, had gone to see him play a few local shows in the past and taken some pictures, which has led to him knowing who she is and getting to talk to him a bit.

We arrive at Poetry Lounge, a small bar in Millvale with a stage in the back corner. Quite a different venue than the last time I saw Anthony play, which was at Stage AE when Badflower was opening for 311. The show started, and immediately, I was blown away by the performance. It was Guitar Zack, an incredibly talented guitar player in the Pittsburgh scene. As a musician myself, I was really impressed by his guitar-playing abilities, his tone, and his stage presence. As I think about many shows, this is not a show that should have 20 people in the audience. Zack is a lot more talented than guitar players I have seen in touring bands at venues like Stage AE. The $5 show was entertaining from beginning until end, including a drum solo that Anthony took halfway through the set.

After the show, we got to talk to Anthony for a little bit. He is connected with my mom and I on social media, and because of that, it was like talking to an old friend you know from the local scene. I ended up staying and talking to him and his friends for quite a while after the show. We talked about local music, open mics, and everything in between.

Alex, the girl he was with, told me that she recognized me, as she had seen Chip & the Charge Ups at North Side Music Festival. The conversations were all sparked by passion for local music. It is evident that her and Anthony are both very involved in the local scene and even met through the scene despite Anthony being a full-time touring musician. It is awesome to be able to talk to a musician you look up to like an old friend.

In a world driven by likes, comments, reposts, and direct messages, most people would be floored by an interaction like this. I have friends who freak out because one of their favorite musicians replied to their comment or messaged them back on Instagram.

Unfortunately, the basis of connection is lost in these scenarios. Talking to Anthony felt like talking to most people in the local scene. He is very down-to-earth and fun to talk to and be around. And this is a prime example of why supporting local music matters so much. You don't know who in the scene may *already* be successful, or who will become successful with their craft.

Regardless of status or fame, everyone in the scene is a talented, interesting human being who puts tons of effort into doing what they do.

- [ ] Dreams
- [ ] Everything is fine
- [ ] Drone Suit
- [ ] Menagerie
- [ ] Vessels
- [ ] Weird fishes.
- [ ] Valley Below
- [ ] Better than that
- [ ] Flood.

*Aliquid Novi setlist*

If you are the kind of person who would freak out about a musician you look up to liking your Instagram post, then the local music scene is a place where you will thrive. The level of talent in local music is the same level of talent you will find playing at Starlake.

Sure, there might be more production, a bigger light show, and a better sound system at Starlake—but the musicians who are playing at these small venues will put on a show that is equally impressive. The tickets are significantly cheaper. The parking lots will be easier to get out of. The musicians will be more accessible to talk to. And you can build authentic lifelong connections and friendships with the most talented people you've ever met.

The connections and friendships you build in the scene are invaluable.

Some local artists may prefer random strangers in the audience to a supporter whom they befriend. At one local show I went to, I noticed that I knew just about every single person in the audience from the music scene. This made me feel excited, because it takes a lot of people who care in order to pack a venue like that. When I had talked to the artist about this, they seemed to have a more negative view of that. This artist would prefer to have random fans rather than people who are already in their life who support them. Personally, anyone filling a room to listen to my music would warm my heart, whether it is 100% strangers or it's every single one of my friends and family members. To me, a packed venue is a packed venue regardless of who is there.

*Especially* because there are so many people out there unwilling to go to support local music—from someone random in another band, to someone you consider to be your best friend.

Talking to many people who felt the need to speak out about their opinion on the music scene, I found that many people live in their own bubble with no concept of a world outside of their own. "Nonexistent music scene" is a phrase I have heard people use. And I always follow up with "well, what was the last local show that you went to?" The answer every single time has been along the lines of "I don't go to local shows." Of course, you will think the local music scene is non-existent if you don't go out to see how much it truly is thriving.

> ***"I think the Pittsburgh music scene is something that's always been there. How closely are you looking at it?"***
>
> **-Sharon Dominick**

The truth is, there can't be a music scene without people who love local musicians. "I think there's a lot that everyone can gain by just being open-minded and seeing what good music might be out there that they may not have heard of yet," says Chip.

Millvale Music Festival received over 800 applications to play their festival in 2026. This means that there are over 800 bands in the area. That is over 800 opportunities to hear something you've never heard before. There's a pretty good possibility that you will like at least *one* of them.

As a musician myself, seeing people from other bands supporting my music matters to me the most of all. In October, Never Say Die played at our annual Halloween Festival, When We Were Dead. There were 7 bands on the festival, all of which I am a huge fan of.

Luckily, we played last, so I had the chance to see every single band play. Our set started at 11pm, later than most festivals or shows typically go.

Looking out into the crowd and seeing the room still being packed was incredible. However, the thing that meant the most to me was seeing members of all the other bands in the audience. Seeing TK from Dream the Heavy dancing to our original music, Jerry from Red Coin taking photos, and so many members of the other bands rocking out to our music warmed my heart.

I had the time of my life dancing and singing along to these bands' music, without worrying if they were going to stay to see our set. I honestly kind of assumed that the venue would empty out towards the end of the night, but thankfully, it didn't at all.

Scenarios like that are the core foundation of the music scene. Making connections with these artists is so important because the scene is for the listeners just as much as it is for the musicians. You won't have one without the other.

These bands are not *just* local bands. These are future Grammy-award winners, future writers of your next favorite song, and musicians who may just go on to change the world.

And if they don't change the world, they are still making damn good music anyways.

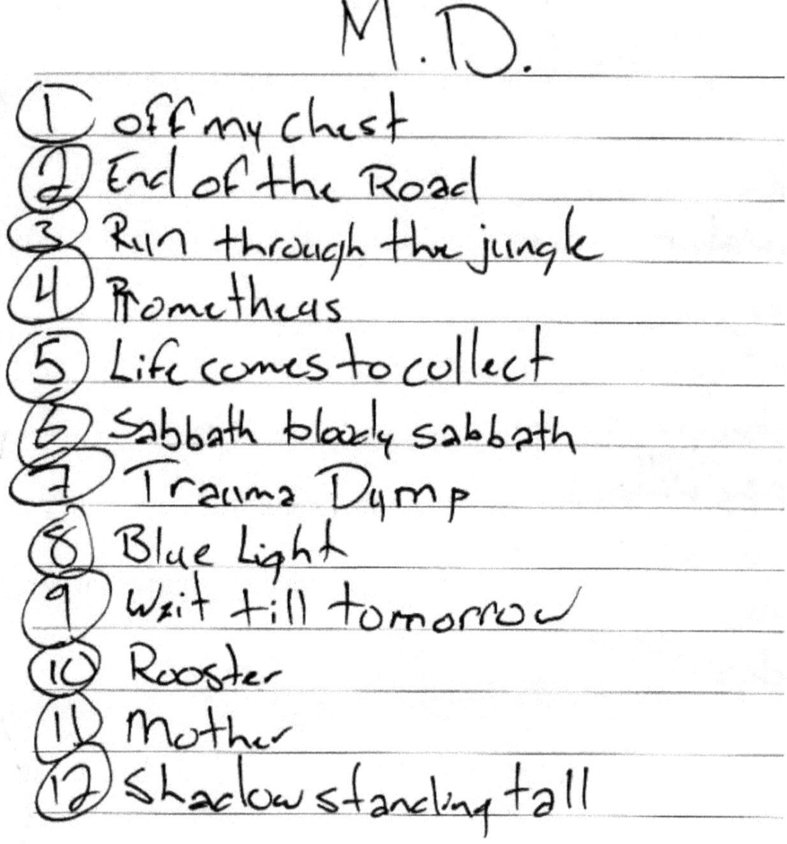


*Morning Dive setlist*

# A NEW PERSPECTIVE

**Don't ask "What can I gain?"**

**Ask "What can I contribute?"**

This is something that may never cross the mind of the average local musician. Though I have only been truly involved in the music scene for the last 8 or 9 years, I have witnessed a lot of complaints. From bands, musicians, and even myself. Whether it is someone who has been in the music scene for longer than I have been alive, or someone who just moved to Pittsburgh, most people agree that it is a tough scene to be in.

One complaint I have heard is "it is so hard to get a gig." Between thousands of bands in the area, and only maybe 30 venues that local bands can actually play at, it truly *is* difficult to get a gig sometimes, especially as a new band. The only way to guarantee a gig with a crowd is if an already established band takes a chance on you to allow you to play with them. Getting a gig is an especially hard task if you are also looking to make any amount of money, which leads to the next complaint…

"We don't get paid enough." I think this complaint is utterly ridiculous. After Millvale Music Festival 2024, there was a small outrage by a few bands on Facebook, complaining about only getting paid ~$50. For an event that requires hundreds, if not thousands, of employees and volunteers to make the event happen at all, $50 is more than I could want just to get to show up and perform at the coolest music festival of the year.

I worked at Mr. Small's for the 2023 Millvale Music Festival, and seeing how much work all of the venue employees, sound people, bartenders, and organizers put in, I was grateful that the festival was able to take place. I helped to set up and tear down the speakers/monitors/sound system for the Butler Street Stage (the one I would end up playing at in 2025), and that was a lot of work with the 5-10 people we had doing just that one task. That doesn't even take into account the other work all of us did, nor does it take into account the 20-some other stages that had to be set up, let alone all of the other jobs that needed to be done.

I'll say this right now. If you are thinking about getting into the local music scene to make some money, you will be disappointed. You can definitely make a few dollars here and there, but there are very few opportunities to make significant amounts of money.

Being a part of the local scene is all for the love of music and performing. A ton of the shows that my bands play are benefit shows. The band doesn't get paid a dime, but it's more than satisfying to play these shows because we love music and are raising money for important causes.

Neverwake has been hosting their annual Halloween benefit festival, Sleepwalkers Ball, for years now. "We have raised money every year that we've done it," says Justin Sanford, guitarist for Neverwake. "To be able to give to children's hospitals has always been pretty rewarding, from being able to go out and have a show and do the rock and roll part of it," says Justin, "but being able to give the donation to the children's hospital has been rewarding." To be able to combine the excitement of getting to play a packed show and the generosity of donating to children's hospitals, there are never any downsides to playing shows like this. Though it is nice when you do get paid to play a show, it is so much more rewarding to play for a good cause. No one at these shows is playing music for any reason other than the joys of performing, and it's an additional benefit that the activity we all enjoy can help fund donations for children's hospitals.

*Justin Sanford of Neverwake at Sleepwalkers Ball 2022*

*Sharon Dominick Photography*

The biggest complaint that I have heard, however, has been "nobody comes to my shows." A complaint I have heard, and a complaint I have made. The oversaturation of bands, shows, and other events going on makes it feel like you must have the perfect marketing strategy to get anyone to even consider coming to your show. But the truth is, no matter how good your marketing strategy is, it's still a really difficult task to get people to come to your shows. So, this is where the "don' what I can gain, ask what I can contribute" mentality matters the most.

What would your ideal supporter look like? The kind of supporter that you want is probably someone who would treat your music in the same way they would treat a nationally touring band. You probably just wish that someone would get *excited* and *enthusiastic* about this art that you've spent hours, if not years, perfecting.

Would they show up to your shows, stand in the front row, and sing every word to your songs? Would they talk to you after the show and compliment you on your performance? Would they post about it when you release new music? Would they wear your band's t-shirt out in public? Would they stream your music and give it a true, focused, thorough listen through?

Here comes the hard question:

**When was the last time you did this for another local band?**

If every Pittsburgh musician did this, I think it could significantly change the entire music scene for the better.

There are so many possibilities to discover new music in Pittsburgh. There is never a weekend without at least a handful of shows check out. "I think people should just go to shows. That's how you discover new stuff. You might find your new favorite band. You might find something you never expected to see," says Jake Curran. "Especially in Pittsburgh. With such a melting pot of music, you can find anything here. You just have to know where to look. When you know where to look, you might find something pretty cool."

When I started researching the local scene in early 2025, I had a very similar mindset to all of these complaints. *Especially* wondering why no one was coming to my shows. It is such a defeating feeling when you play to empty room after empty room, wondering if anyone will ever care about the art you've poured your soul into. However, in writing this book, I found an entirely new perspective on the music scene.

I have always been and will always be a music enjoyer above all else. This is the mindset that I needed to have while navigating the music scene all along. Because along the way, I got caught up in wondering why no one cares, and forgot that I am doing this music thing out of pure love and adoration for the art. Not only do I enjoy writing music and performing, but I love listening. I have been a fangirl of different bands and artists practically since the day I was born. The only reason I am a musician is because I was first a music fan. That is who I had to become again.

*Cody Kulesa and Nolan Allen*

*Sharon Dominick Photography*

Doing research for this book consisted of two things: talking to local musicians and going to local shows. For research purposes, I decided I was going to try to go to as many local shows as I could to observe. And the biggest conclusion that I drew from my research is that Pittsburgh music is *fucking* incredible.

I already knew this just from seeing all the other bands at shows I have played, and from going to local festivals. But taking the research approach highlighted this excellence even more than I had ever noticed before.

At first, I did this because I wanted to be a supporter of local music, and along the way, I became a fan. I have been a supporter for many years, going to shows every once in a while, or watching the performers at the AcoustiCafe open mic. This summer, I became a fan—just like one might become a fan of Taylor Swift, My Chemical Romance, Morgan Wallen, or whoever else is popular right now. I went to see Ferocious Ghosts, Old Neon, Aliquid Novi, Broom, Amy Mmhmm, Jaaye, The Vics, KGVSUNIVERSE, Dream the Heavy, and Nathan King—to name just a few. I always tried to get to the front row, always sang along to the songs I knew, and tried to cheer louder than anyone else in the room. Being a local music fan is mutually beneficial to both the fan and the musician. The musician gets to see their art being fully appreciated, and the fan gets to have a front-row experience seeing a band or artist that they love.

We all know people who love to brag about getting to see a band in a small venue before they blew up. I know I have done it a lot. When I saw Sleeping With Sirens play at Starlake, all I could think about was how I had seen them play at The Altar Bar—a 650 capacity venue—ten years prior. I would much rather see a band I love at a small, intimate venue than at a 15,000+ capacity venue. Every band you've ever loved is just a local band that got their music listened to by major record labels.

"We were so excited when we saw your message about buying a ticket for the show," Noah Goisse, singer of Broom, said after a show. They were the local opener for a national act at Jergel's that night, and I had gone to the show to specifically see them. "It's like that's *our* person that we got to come to the show!" In this moment, I knew I was officially a fan, and not just someone who knows the band. It hadn't even crossed my mind that my presence at this show to see them would make a difference. I just wanted to see one of my favorite bands play.

*I had done what I set out to do: I became the fan I wish I had.*

**CHALLENGE:**

**Find a local artist who moves you the same way your favorite touring bands do. Fully immerse yourself in the local scene—go to shows, listen intentionally, and keep searching until you find at least one band or artist who wins your heart.**

Not only did my presence in the scene matter, but it also started to cause exponential growth. I started by going to shows by myself. Then I'd bring one friend. Then two or three. And all of the people that I brought to shows started bringing other people. Though I may only show up with a group of 4-6 people at a show, those people then in turn invite their friends for the next show.

After I had become the fan I wish I had, I also started to see that community come back and support me just as I had supported them. Members of Aliquid Novi were showing up to my acoustic sets. Members of Old Neon were coming to see Chip & the Charge Ups. At one Charge Ups show, all the members of Broom showed up with cardboard cutouts of our faces! Seeing them in the front row holding up my own face was an unbelievable experience. I hadn't even asked for this support, yet it was a direct result of me showing them my support. When I went to these bands' shows and streamed their music, I wasn't doing it with the intention of receiving anything in return.

*Ben, Caleb, Carter and Noah from Broom*

*Sharon Dominick Photography*

I had stopped caring about who supported me and started focusing on how I could support others. I thought that the result of me going to these shows was simply that I got to see a killer show, but it turned out to be a bigger moment for connections to be made. That was just the natural consequence of being a fan who is also a musician.

For years, I had tried to figure out how to get people to come to my shows. I'd seen so many musicians fall into the "I'll support you *only* if you support me first" mindset, then wonder why they never felt supported. However, when I stopped chasing validation and simply poured genuine love into the music in the scene, I ended up getting the support they'd been searching for—without having to even ask for it.

The transactional mentality needs to end if the community wants to grow and progress collectively.

"Do things *from* love, not *for* love"—a phrase I have heard many times and have realized how much it applies to communities just like this one. I started supporting bands simply because I love the music. You have my back, and I'll have yours. You come to my shows, and I'll come to yours. And if you don't? I will still be there anyways.

## My love for music is unconditional.

The Pittsburgh music scene existed long before me, and it will continue long after I'm gone. The music scene is a living, thriving organism—if you love it, care for it, and nurture it, it will return the favor to you. But if you neglect it, it will leave you feeling neglected. So, get out in the scene, enjoy local music, support the musicians, and experience the incredible music community that Pittsburgh has to offer.

www.ingramcontent.com/pod-product-compliance
Lightning Source LLC
LaVergne TN
LVHW010903110826
845149LV00005B/1450

*9781257566693*